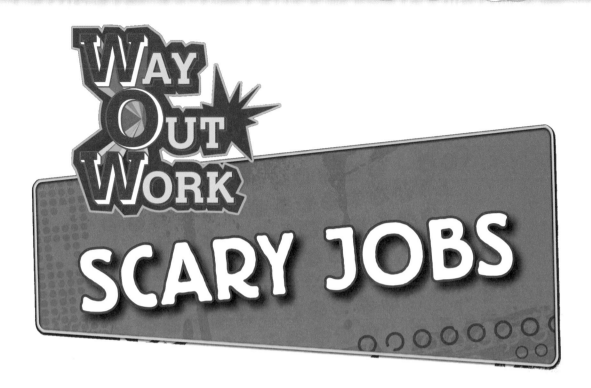

Diane Lindsey Reeves

Ferguson
An imprint of Infobase Publishing

Acknowledgements

Special thanks to Tamiko Bogad, Tony Hawk, Nicholas Patrick, Debi Radisch, and Duane Ross for sharing the stories behind their courageous work. A huge thank you to Joy Strickland, research assistant extraordinaire, whose ideas and hard work added so much to this series.

Way Out Work: Scary Jobs

Copyright © 2009 by Diane Lindsey Reeves

Ferguson
An imprint of Infobase Publishing, Inc.
132 West 31st Street
New York, NY 10001

Library of Congress Cataloging-in-Publication Data
Reeves, Diane Lindsey, 1959–
  Scary jobs / Diane Lindsey Reeves. — 1st ed.
      p. cm. — (Way out work)
  Includes index.
  ISBN-13: 978-1-60413-128-4 (hardcover : alk. paper)
  ISBN-10: 1-60413-128-4 (hardcover : alk. paper) 1. Work. 2. Professions. 3. Risk-taking
(Psychology) I. Title.
  HD4901.R43 2009
  331.702—dc22

                              2008054420

Ferguson books are available at special discounts when purchased in bulk quantities for businesses, associations, institutions, or sales promotions. Please call our Special Sales Department in New York at (212) 967-8800 or (800) 322-8755. You can find Ferguson on the World Wide Web at http://www.fergpubco.com

Text design by Erika K. Arroyo
Cover design by Jooyoung An

Printed in the United States of America

Bang FOF 10 9 8 7 6 5 4 3 2 1

This book is printed on acid-free paper.

Contents

Introduction

There's *scary* and then there's *SCARY*. Scary is first day of school jitters. It's that spine-tingling, "Am I having fun yet?" panic you feel when you ride a rollercoaster or visit a haunted house. It's that "jump out of your skin" freak-out you get when watching a creepy movie on TV.

SCARY is blasting off in a spaceship bound for out-of-this-world destinations. SCARY is coming to work one day, finding your office full of the victims of a horrible accident, and having to find out what the heck happened and why they died. SCARY is flying into the eye of a hurricane, crossing your fingers, and hoping to come out safely on the other side.

SCARY is what some people do for a living, day in and day out. What do they do? How do they do it? And why in the world would they—or you—want to? Answers to these questions and more are coming your way as you start reading about some of the scariest jobs in the world.

Along with introducing what each job is really like, the job articles in this book include several interesting features to get you thinking in new and unexpected ways. Then get ready for more scary job ideas and stop by to read about a few people who do scary stuff for a living. Make sure to spend a little time at the end of the book, where you can play around with some activities and find out once and for all if you've got the guts to do what these people do.

Astronaut

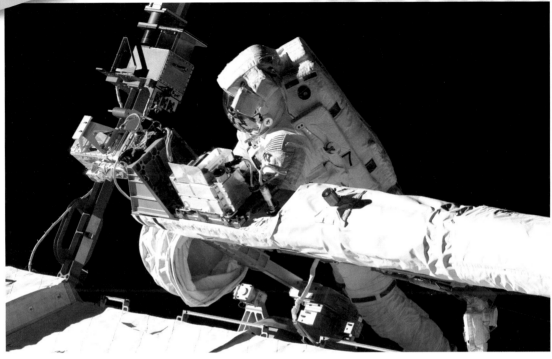

Astronaut Mike Foreman, STS-123 mission specialist, helps tie down the Orbiter Boom Sensor System on the International Space Station. *UPI/Landov*

So far, only 321 of America's top scientists, engineers, and pilots have had the "right stuff" to become astronauts since NASA (National Aeronautics and Space Administration) got its start in 1958, according to Duane Ross, NASA manager of astronaut candidate selection and training. About 88 astronauts are currently training for a coveted spot aboard the Space Shuttle or at the International Space Station.

These fortunate few, the best of the best, were chosen by NASA because they had solid academic backgrounds in engineering, math, or science, interesting work experience, and outside interests that showed they had an ability to adapt to different situations. Sometimes, with so many well-qualified candidates to choose from, the final decision boiled down to how nice they were. Nice, as in how would you like to spend a few weeks cooped up in a space capsule with this person?

Once selected, astronauts spend years training for the couple of weeks or months they will ultimately spend in space. And they don't call this stuff rocket science for nothing. The training process is challenging all the way around—intellectually, physically, and mentally. Astronauts have to be ready to respond to every imaginable "what if" situation in space. After all, if something goes wrong, it's not like they can count on a local space alien for help.

So, astronaut training is definitely an intense process. But scary?

Scary starts at liftoff with astronauts suited up and buckled in. Below

Scare Factor
Going places few humans dare to go.

them enormous engines fire up, solid rocket boosters start burning through nearly 500 tons of fuel, and the spacecraft begins hurtling above the earth at a speed of 4,620 miles per hour. And that's just two minutes into the mission!

Although you won't find taking space walks, doing space-age science experiments, and orbiting the earth on most people's daily to-do lists, they are a piece of cake compared to liftoff and reentry dangers. Reentering earth's atmosphere involves speeds in excess of 15,000 miles per hour and spacecraft surface temperatures

Did you know that astronauts can't burp in space? And it's not just because they have good manners. Burps happen when too much air builds up in the stomach. Since there's no gravity in space, there's no burping either, because gas in the digestive system doesn't rise upward.

What Do You Think?
Will people ever live in space?
Would you want to if
you could?

reaching up to 2,300° F. To say such conditions are dangerous would be quite an understatement.

That's where the brain power of some of the other 18,000 or so NASA employees—working at the Kennedy Space Center in Florida, Johnson Space Center in Texas, Marshall Space Flight Center in Ala-bama, and seven other U.S. locations—comes into play. Through the years, and, sadly, as a result of some tragic lessons learned, NASA scientists and engineers have developed incredible technologies, materials, and procedures that make it possible for astronauts to continue to explore the vast frontiers of outer space—and come home to tell the world about it. Currently, the NASA team is working on an awesome new spacecraft for the future called *Orion*.

Ready to take it for a spin? 10, 9, 8...Blast off!

GO FOR IT IF. . .
Curiosity is the name of your game.

You are allergic to learning.

FORGET ABOUT IT IF. . .

Go Online to Find Out More!
Go straight to the source for all your out-of-this-world news at http://kids.msfc.nasa.gov.

Bomb Squad Technician

A bomb squad member investigates a mock suspicious vehicle during a terrorism drill run by the U.S. Department of Homeland Security. *AP Photo/Elise Amendola*

A bad day usually starts with a frantic phone call to the police. For instance, someone found a suspicious-looking backpack left beneath a subway seat. Or, even worse, someone calls to say, "Hey, by the way, I just left a bomb somewhere in town and I sure hope you find it before it goes off."

Now the backpack could be full of some careless kid's homework or it could be full of dangerous explosives. And that phone call could be from a goofball trying to get attention or it could be from an evil person intent on doing harm. But there's too much

Kaboom! Say that word and you'll know how long it takes for a bomb squad technician's day to go from good to really, really bad.

What Do You Think?
What do you suppose bomb squad techs think about when they make that long walk between safety and an explosive device?

Scare Factor

Proximity to explosive devices!

at stake to guess and there's only one way to find out for sure.

It's time to do two things: Clear the area and call the bomb squad. Fortunately, bomb squad technicians have lots of high-tech tools to help keep them (and the rest of the world) safe. If it becomes necessary to get up close and personal with the suspicious device, they suit up in protective gear. This gear weighs about 80 pounds, is made of the same type of super-strong Kevlar material as bulletproof vests, and includes an extra-heavy duty helmet and face guard. Think of what it would be like to clean your very messy room if you were dressed from head to toe in a bulky snowsuit and gloves and you'll have an idea of what it's like to wear this lifesaving gear.

Bomb squad technicians also use listening devices that work just like the stethoscope your doctor uses to listen to your heart and special X-ray machines to examine suspicious packages. In situations where a threat has been made but the bomb's exact location is unknown, specially trained dogs may be used to help sniff out the explosives.

If it turns out that the only thing in the backpack is a bunch of books and a leftover bologna sandwich or if every inch of a targeted building is searched and no bomb is found, everyone breathes a big sigh of relief and goes on about their business. If, instead, they discover the tick, tick, tick of a detonator timer, they have to work ever-so-quickly and oh-so-carefully to disable the bomb on the spot.

WOW!

Bomb disposal robots are getting smarter all the time. Whenever possible, robots are used to find bombs and defuse them. Some robots, used in military conflicts, can even be used to move injured people out of harm's way.

GO FOR IT IF...

You can think fast and have nerves of steel.

- - - - - - - - - - - - - -

Your hands shake and your knees knock together just thinking about bombs.

FORGET ABOUT IT IF...

Or they place the bomb in a containment vessel and move it somewhere safe to blow it up. In some cases, robots do the dirty work of tracking and disabling bombs.

Once again, it's training to the rescue. Bomb squad technicians stay cool in these very scary situations because they've practiced (and practiced and practiced) exactly what they have to do. Still, it takes a lot of skill and a special kind of courage to do what bomb squad technicians do.

Go Online to Find Out More!

Put some hazardous duty robots to work at http://www.pbs.org/wgbh/nova/robots.

Disease Detective

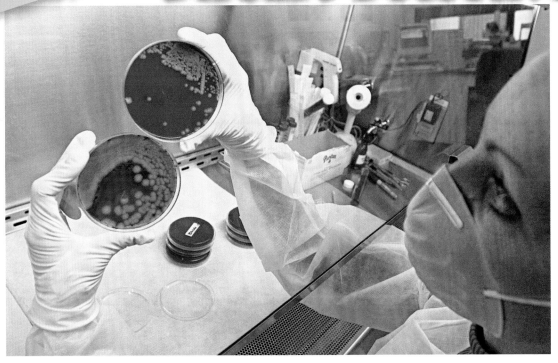

Senior microbiologist Cheryl Gauthier displays petri dishes containing bacteria samples at the Department of Public Health state laboratory in Boston. *AP Photo/Elise Amendola*

The year was 1854. The place was London, England. The problem was a cholera outbreak. People were dropping like flies from this dreadful, highly contagious disease. At the time, most doctors thought that cholera germs spread through the air. But one doctor, Dr. John Snow, had another idea. He started mapping out where people who caught the disease lived. Hot on the trail of a common source of infection, he found out where each patient got his or her water. After a meticulous investigation that would have made Sherlock Holmes proud, he discovered that a specific water pump on a specific street was where many of the victims were being infected. He had the handle of the pump removed and, presto, the epidemic was stopped in its tracks. Little did Dr. Snow know that, because of his tireless sleuthing, he would forever be known as the father of epidemiology.

Epidemiology is the fancy scientific name for a type of medical research that involves tracking down the sources and causes of diseases that affect public health. This includes diseases that challenge the entire world, such as AIDS, hepatitis, and the flu. Disease detectives also investigate public health problems on a smaller scale, like when a bunch of people get sick after eating at a certain restaurant. Some work on public health issues like the obesity epidemic and diseases related to lifestyle choices such as tobacco use.

Disease detectives are highly trained doctors even though some of the methods they use are very sim-

Scare Factor
Close encounters with deadly diseases.

ilar to those used by law-enforcement detectives. Of course, the bad guys they go after aren't your typical crooks and robbers. They're germs, such as bacteria and flu viruses, and other sources of health threats that menace the public. Similar to their crime-fighting counterparts, disease detectives look for clues, collect evidence, and try to crack each case by finding answers to important questions such as who has the disease, where do they live, when did they get it, what caused it, and most importantly, how can we stop it from spreading.

WOW!

Guess what the most effective tool used to investigate disease mysteries is. Hint #1: It's not high-tech. Hint #2: You've probably got one and use it regularly. Answer: It's a mouth. Disease detectives use theirs to ask lots and lots of questions.

The Centers for Disease Control and Prevention (CDC) is an important national agency dedicated to fighting disease in much the same way that the Federal Bureau of Investigation (FBI) works to fight crime. The CDC is where many of the nation's top disease detectives get their training and where many of them work. It's also where public health officials from all over the world come to learn how to keep themselves safe from the diseases they investigate by taking precautions like wearing masks and gloves.

Of course, the best part of being a disease detective is that sometimes

What Do You Think?

How do you think disease detectives keep from getting the diseases they are investigating?

their work helps other doctors and scientists figure out how to totally wipe out certain diseases with special vaccines. That was exactly what happened in the case of the diseases polio and tuberculosis, which once ran rampant throughout the world. Disease detectives hope that someday soon, the same thing will be said about diseases like AIDS, influenza, and maybe even the common cold.

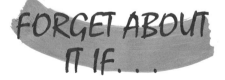

GO FOR IT IF. . .

You like the idea of mixing medicine with sleuthing.

You've got a thing about germs.

FORGET ABOUT IT IF. . .

Go Online to Find Out More!

See if you can stop the most dangerous woman in America before it's too late at http://www.pbs.org/ wgbh/nova/typhoid.

Extreme Sports Pro

Gold-medal winner Travis Pastrana defies gravity while competing in the freestyle motocross during the 2002 Gravity Games in Cleveland, Ohio. *AP Photo/Elyria Chronicle Telegram, Haraz Ghanbari*

BMX racing. Skydiving. Snowboarding. Mountain biking. Surfing. Some people do these extreme sports just for the thrill of it. Others do it for a paycheck too. Extreme sports are just what you'd imagine something described as extreme would be. Extremely fast. Extremely dangerous. Extremely difficult to master. And, when done right, extremely awesome to watch.

Most extreme sports are at least indirectly related to a more mainstream sport. For instance, rollerskating is a mainstream sport; inline skating and skateboarding are more, um, extreme versions of the sport.

What Do You Think?
Why do you suppose some people are more interested in extreme sports while others are more into traditional sports like baseball and soccer?

Scare Factor
You can get hurt doing this stuff!

The difference can best be explained by a characteristic shared by all extreme sports: wildly daring acrobatic stunts performed while traveling at high speeds. Bottom line, extreme sports pros not only have to be amazing athletes, they have to be fearless daredevils as well.

They have to be creative innovators too. One of the reasons extreme sports keeps gaining in popularity—and in pushing the limits of athletic competition—is that advances in sports equipment technology make it possible to do what sometimes would seem impossible. You name the sport and you'll find that the equipment it takes to play it is lighter, tougher, faster, more flexible, and even smarter than ever before. Even athletic shoes and underwear are specially designed by sports equipment engineers to give extreme athletes an extra edge.

Unlike most traditional sports, these sports aren't played in the comfort of cushy stadiums or climate-controlled arenas. The more rugged the terrain, the better for many of the sports classified as extreme. Like an old song says, there "ain't no mountain high enough, ain't no valley low enough" to keep some extreme sports pros away. Some extreme sports, like skateboarding, have gotten so popular that many public parks have special areas where even amateur skateboarders can do their thing to their heart's content (at their own risk, of course!).

According to a survey conducted by the Sporting Goods Manufacturing Association in 2006, the three most popular extreme sports are inline skating (16.4 million participants), skateboarding (11.3 million participants), and paintballing (10.3 millions participants).

GO FOR IT IF . . .

You want to test the limits of your courage and physical abilities.

- - - - - - - - - - - - -

Your worst grade is in P.E.

FORGET ABOUT IT IF . . .

Another way extreme sports are different from traditional ones like football and baseball is that competition tends to be between individuals instead of teams. And it's a good thing that making money is not necessarily the goal of a lot of extreme sports pros because the big bucks don't flow quite as freely in these sports as they do with the big three—football, baseball, and basketball. At least not yet...

Of course, the growing popularity of the X Games may change all that before you know it. The X Games bring the best of the best extreme sports pros from all over the world together twice a year for intense and very entertaining competition.

Success at this level often goes a long way to help competitors make the leap from doing extreme sports for fun to doing it for profit. Aggressively pursuing opportunities to endorse products, competing in tournaments, and making appearances on TV shows and commercials are some of the ways people make their sport work for them. Others support their habit by teaching others how to do what they do—whether it's teaching skiing lessons at a ski resort, leading white-water rafting expeditions, or whatever it takes to keep them in the game and in the money.

Go Online to Find Out More!
Get the latest extreme sports news at http://expn.go.com.

Forensic Pathologist

Forensic scientist Deborah Newville examines stains on a coat held in evidence at the state forensic lab in Portland, Oregon. *AP Photo/Greg Wahl-Stephens*

Forensic pathologists are the last doctors some people ever see. That's because the patients forensic pathologists treat are already dead. They are visiting a forensic pathologist because they died under unusual circumstances, and it's the pathologist's job to find out why.

If you've ever watched one of those popular crime shows on TV like *CSI*, *Crossing Jordan*, or *Law and Order*, you may have seen a forensic pathologist in action. On those shows, whenever someone gets murdered or killed in an accident, they end up lying on a slab in the county morgue. The forensic pathologist comes in to conduct what amounts to an investigation of the cause of death. For once, TV gets it right and the forensic pathologists'

work on these shows is pretty close to what they do in real life—minus all the drama in their personal lives, of course. On TV, as in any medical examiner's office, the forensic pathologist starts his or her investigations by running different kinds of medical tests, making careful notes, and performing autopsies.

Autopsies are like head-to-toe surgery where pathologists carefully examine every square inch of a person's body—inside and out. By the time the examination is complete, a pathologist knows more than most people would willingly share about that person's health and lifestyle habits—including the contents of their last meal. They should know why someone died and in the case of violent deaths, how it happened. The last thing they do is file a report that indicates whether the cause of death was natural, accidental, suicide, or homicide. The reporting process often takes much more time than the actual physical investigation because the pathologist must be certain to record every detail to back up their conclusions.

Of course, not every patient who happens by the forensic laboratory is the victim of a violent crime or accident. Sometimes forensic pathologists are asked to find out why someone who seemed healthy enough one minute dropped dead the next. They can determine if the person suddenly suffered a heart attack, stroke,

The New York City Medical Examiner's office used sophisticated DNA testing methods to try to identify remains from the 2,749 people known to have been killed in the terrorist attacks on the World Trade Center. Even so, only 1,585, or 58 percent of the victims, have been identified so far.

What Do You Think?
What is the worst way to die?
Hint: Things like fires and airplane crashes are high on a lot of people's lists.

or some other fatal condition. They also determine cause of death when someone dies while under medical care, perhaps as a result of surgery or taking the wrong medication.

One more thing you might want to know is that forensic patholo-

GO FOR IT IF...

You've got an especially strong stomach and like to solve mysteries.

- - - - - - - - - - - - - -

You freak out at the sight of blood.

FORGET ABOUT IT IF...

gists are also sometimes called coroners or medical examiners. And, one thing they'd like you to know is that their work isn't as creepy as it might seem, and they aren't ghouls who like hanging around dead people. They are problem-solvers who speak up for people who can't speak for themselves. As surprising as it might seem, dead bodies aren't the scariest part of this job. Having to tell people how someone they loved has died sometimes takes far more courage.

Go Online to Find Out More!

Find out how autopsies are conducted at http:// health.howstuffworks. com/autopsy.htm. *Warning:* Pictures of a real autopsy may gross you out.

Smokejumper

Smokejumper Larry Wilson leaps from a DC-3TP airplane during training. *Darin Oswald/ MCT/Landov*

As if running into burning buildings like most firefighters do isn't scary enough, how about jumping out of an airplane into a raging forest fire? That's exactly what smokejumpers, a tough bunch of highly trained firefighters, do to fight wild fires. As scary as it sounds, the alternative is to hike miles through dense woods with mules being the only viable form of transportation available to lug supplies. Along with not being much fun, this ineffective method also

What Do You Think?
Why are there more forest fires in the Western states than in other parts of the U.S.?

20

gives raging fires way too much time to wreak havoc.

This is why every summer elite teams of smokejumpers load themselves, their parachutes, their tools, and their personal gear into small airplanes or helicopters and head toward the flames. Of course, that first step out of the airplane can be a doozy, and sometimes firefighters find themselves stuck up in a tree, gusting with the wind to the wrong place, or landing just a little too close to the fire for comfort. Smokejumpers are trained to deal with situations like these and in no time they are digging trenches and clearing vegetation to cut off the fire from its fuel sources.

You didn't think they'd pull a fire hose and water hydrant out of their backpack, did you? No, fighting forest fires is a lot different than fighting fires in a city where water is the firefighting weapon of choice. Fighting forest fires involves vastly different skills and incredible amounts of physical stamina. After all, once the smokejumpers take that first leap, they are stuck in the woods until the fire is out, whether it takes hours, days, or weeks. The fact that there is no comfy fire station to bunk in after a hard day's work (they camp out under the stars instead) is just one more way that smokejumpers go the extra mile to keep the world safe.

Fires are unpredictable. Add acres of burning trees and a little wind and you've got the makings of a very

WOW!

It takes three elements to create a fire: fuel, oxygen, and heat. These three ingredients are called the fire triangle.

GO FOR IT IF. . .

You want a double dose of adventure with your work.

- - - - - - - - - - - -

Camping out in remote areas isn't your thing.

FORGET ABOUT IT IF. . .

combustible situation. And that's no joke. It doesn't take much for a smokejumper to get trapped in an inferno. One of the most important things they have to do is keep escape routes in mind at all times. When all else fails and smokejumpers can't escape, they are taught to lie flat on the ground, cover themselves with

flame-resistant blankets, and hope for the best until the fire moves on.

Smokejumpers are specially trained firefighters who work on call during the hot summer months, which, due to soaring temperatures, dry climates, lightning strikes, and careless campers, are prime time for forest fires. During this season, a jumper might fight five to 15 fires in different parts of the country. Keep in mind that not just any firefighter can be a smokejumper. In fact, there are only about 400 smokejumpers in the entire United States!

Go Online to Find Out More!
See what Smokey Bear has to say about forest fires at http://www.smokey bear.com.

Skywalker

A skywalker welds a skyscraper in Chicago. *Craig Aurness/Corbis*

Sure, using a flame-throwing torch to weld thick pieces of metal together could get a bit dangerous if you weren't careful, but is it scary? Professional welders do it without incident every day in all kinds of factories, manufacturing plants, and building sites.

But, here's the thing: Skywalkers are a special breed of steel worker who perform their welding tasks in skyscrapers. And what's the big deal about that? First of all, the skyscrapers are still under construction. And—drum roll, please—the skyscrapers don't have floors yet! To get an idea

What Do You Think?
Why do you suppose the invention of elevators made it possible for skyscrapers to go higher and higher?

of what this is like, imagine spending your entire day at school standing on a high balance beam. Kind of tricky, don't you think?

The sky has truly been the limit since the first skyscraper was erected in Chicago back in 1885. Standing nine stories high, the building made history and paved the way for big cities to get even bigger by going up instead of out to make room for more people to live and work.

But, even the tallest skyscrapers start from the ground up. And it's up to skywalkers to build the super structure that holds everything together. By riveting together huge steel beams that run both horizontally and vertically, they create a huge steel skeleton or grid. It all starts underground in the substructure and continues upward, floor by floor by floor, all the way to the top—whether it's 10 stories or (gulp!) more than 100.

A couple of things make this process a little easier and a whole lot safer. First is the safety gear skywalkers use—things like scaffolding, harnesses, and lifelines help keep them up where they belong. It also helps that the higher the superstructure gets, the more opportunity other workers have to work below them on handy little niceties like walls and floors.

Even though the Petronas Towers in Kuala Lumpur, Malaysia, were long hailed as the world's tallest buildings at 1,483 feet, and are 33 feet taller than the Sears Tower in Chicago, Illinois, the Sears Tower's usable space actually goes 200 feet higher. But, who's counting? Now the Dubai Tower in the United Arab Emirates towers over both at 1,985 feet, with 159 completed floors as of early 2008, and more to come.

GO FOR IT IF. . .

You like the idea of working with your hands, building amazing buildings, and are up (really up!) for a job where you can't look down.

- - - - - - - - - - - - - -

You have two left feet or are afraid of heights!

FORGET ABOUT IT IF. . .

There's still no getting around the fact that this is not a typical job or an ordinary worksite. Doing it right requires a delicate balancing act (no pun intended!) of professional weld- ing skill and the physical prowess of an acrobat.

Of course, if working at high altitudes doesn't quite cut it, welders can always plunge in for some deep-sea welding. That's right. Some welders are also commercial divers who work underwater on oil rigs, bridge supports, and ships. Like their sky-high counterparts, underwater welders have to be extremely good at what they do in order to handle working in such dangerous environments.

Go Online to Find Out More!

Become a skyscraper whiz at http://www.pbs. org/wgbh/buildingbig/ skyscraper/index.html.

Scary Job #8

Spy

A spy uses binoculars to watch her target. *Tim McConville/zefa/Corbis*

Spies play make-believe for a living. At least, that's what it may seem like on the surface. But espionage (the fancy name for spying) is anything but fun and games. Yes, spies often have to pretend to be someone else, and, yes, they sometimes wear disguises and get to use really cool tools to do their job. But the secrets they are trying to uncover are quite often a matter of life and death.

The Central Intelligence Agency (CIA) is in charge of gathering intelligence (or important secrets about other governments) from around the

What Do You Think?
In what, if any, circumstances do you think it would be okay to lie in order to get important national security information?

world that helps the United States government keep its citizens and international allies (or friends) safe. But working as a CIA agent today involves a lot more than the cloak and dagger stuff you see on TV.

Intelligence agents rely on some amazing technologies to seek out top secret information all over the world. Most often the information spies are trying to uncover is of a political or military nature. In other words, it's big, high-stakes, "lots of people could get hurt if we don't stop this" stuff.

In reality, a CIA spy is just as likely to be a scientist, engineer, economist, linguist, mathematician, secretary, accountant, or computer specialist as they are a field agent. Together, these professionals acquire enormous amounts of information every day, in every language known to mankind, from every corner of the world. This vast array of information comes through spying as well as from newspapers, Internet searches, eavesdropping on important meetings in foreign lands, and images from super-sophisticated satellites. Sorting through it and deciding what's most important is as much a part of the job as sleuthing.

Since the 9/11 terrorists attacks, the Federal Bureau of Investigation (FBI) also helps "to protect and defend

WOW!

Cryptology is the science of hiding information. Spies use it to pass along secret messages in codes and ciphers. But, did you know that you use it too? Yep, you use it every time you (or your parents) type in a computer password or use an ATM card.

GO FOR IT IF . . .

You think you have a lot in common with James Bond.

- - - - - - - - - - - - - - -

You can't keep a secret!

FORGET ABOUT IT IF . . .

the United States against terrorist and foreign intelligence threats," in addition to providing a wide range of criminal justice services worldwide, especially to national, state, and local government agencies. Like CIA agents, FBI agents tend to be highly specialized, very smart, and ready to do what it takes to keep the world safe.

Closer to home, you'll find undercover agents working at local law-enforcement agencies to catch criminals involved in bad stuff like drugs, gangs, and organized crime. Sometimes they have to go undercover and pretend to be someone else in order to get close enough to find out who's doing what and to gather evidence of the wrongdoer's crimes. In these situations, undercover agents have to be extra careful to protect their real identities and to totally fake out the criminals by convincing them that they don't care how bad the criminal may be.

Bottom line, when it comes to spying there are lots of ways to go undercover, whether it's across town or on the other side of the world.

Go Online to Find Out More!
Play around at the International Spy Museum at http://www.spymuseum. org/programs/games.php.

Stormchaser

Stormchasers study a severe thunderstorm in Kansas. *Jim Reed/Corbis*

Think fast! You're at the beach. Rain is pounding like a million jackhammers turned loose at once. Waves are surging up to ridiculously wild heights. Wind is raging at more than 74 miles per hour (mph), which, by the way, is faster than your parents can safely drive a car on a highway. Where would you rather be: huddled inside the safest room you can find in your house or sitting in the cockpit of a weather reconnaissance airplane flying through the middle of the storm?

If you happen to be a stormchaser, there's no place you'd rather be than right smack in the middle of things, and, oddly enough, you may be safer there than on the ground. Here's why: Hurricanes are shaped like donuts with the outside ring being where the wind and rain swirl and whirl, unleashing all kinds of fury. Meteo-

29

rologists, or weather scientists, call the inside part of the hurricane—the donut hole—the eye of the storm. Things there are relatively calm, so it's where stormchasers aboard special airplanes go to conduct research experiments that let them know how fast the hurricane is moving, how strong it is, and where it is headed. Of course, actually getting in and out of the eye is a challenge in and of itself.

Hurricanes keep stormchasers who work near the Atlantic Ocean busy from June to November each year. But it's tornados, another type of violent weather condition, that keeps stormchasers hopping in "Tornado Alley" during the spring months of April through June. Tornado Alley includes states located between the Mississippi River and the high plains like Texas, Oklahoma, Kansas, Nebraska, Iowa, Missouri, Arkansas, and Louisiana. Other states are not exempt from tornados but they aren't as common as in this area.

A tornado is defined as a violently rotating column of air extending from a thunderstorm to the ground. The most violent tornados are capable of tremendous destruction with wind speeds of 250 mph or more. Damage paths can be in excess of one

Tornados are classified as weak when they last one to 10 minutes with winds less than 110 mph, strong when they last more than 20 minutes with winds between 110 and 205 mph, and violent when they last more than an hour with winds over 205 mph. On the other hand, hurricanes are classified on a scale of one to five, with one being the mildest and five considered catastrophic.

mile wide and 50 miles long. The weird thing about tornados is that, even though they accompany severe rainstorms, things often get eerily quiet right before they hit. But you'll know it's time to duck for cover (in a basement or inside room without windows) when the sky turns an icky shade of green and it starts to sound like a freight train is roaring through.

Both types of stormchasers rely on modern technology to help them do their job. Information from satellites and special radars helps them identify and track storm systems as they develop. Sophisticated weather warning systems help alert people to the dangers headed their way.

With an average of 800 tornados per year and five to 15 major hurricanes, stormchasers everywhere stay busy trying to keep one step ahead of nasty weather patterns.

GO FOR IT IF...

You are a total weather buff.

- - - - - - - - - - - - - - - -

You'd rather watch weather disasters on TV than experience them firsthand.

FORGET ABOUT IT IF...

Stunt Person

Stunt doubles for stars Harrison Ford and Shia LaBeouf ride a motorcycle while filming *Indiana Jones and the Kingdom of the Crystal Skull.* *Bobby Bank/WireImage*

Look out! Did you see that? That guy just jumped out of the courthouse window. Now he pushed that old man out of his wheelchair and is using it to race down the courthouse steps. Oh no! Did you see him slug that taxi driver? He's now driving off in the taxicab, right up the sidewalk and through the city square. Whoa! What's going on?

You're scrambling to find your cell phone to dial 911 when you hear someone shout "Cut!"

Whew! What you just saw wasn't real. It's a scene from a new action movie and that bad guy isn't some crazed criminal; he's a stunt person acting out a daring scene. Action movies are full of scenes that call for physically demanding and, some-

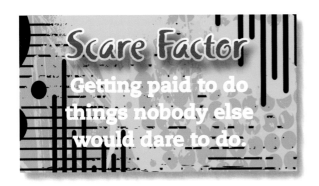

Scare Factor

Getting paid to do things nobody else would dare to do.

times, downright dangerous situations. To avoid endangering the lives and limbs of movie stars, who might find the idea of dangling from a rope attached to a helicopter in flight or engaging in a full-fledged fistfight with a few wannabe gangsters a bit beyond their acting abilities, stunt doubles stand in their place.

Using stunt people for these kinds of scenes achieves two purposes. First, expensive Hollywood productions cannot afford to risk endangering high-priced stars, so using stunt people allows actors to stay safe

between close-ups. Second, it's just easier to use someone who already knows how to do things like high-speed car chases, skydiving, or some other extraordinary skill than to try to teach an actor to do it.

Notice the emphasis on the word skill. Stunt people (and they can be either men or women) aren't just thrill-seeking daredevils, even though some of what they do is definitely thrilling and most certainly daring. Instead, they are highly trained professionals who have learned how to do things that other people would never dare try, and they do it safely and with spectacular results.

Like other kinds of performers, they do what they do to entertain others in movies, commercials, and television shows. Unlike actors, they don't get acting jobs because of their looks, voice, or great personality. It doesn't

One of the most famous movie stunts was filmed in 1928 in *Steamboat Bill, Jr.* In the film, comedian Buster Keaton narrowly ecapes becoming a human pancake when a prop designed to look like a house falls on him. Lucky for him, the attic window fit neatly around his body.

What Do You Think?
Who is your favorite action star? What would you have to do to stand in for them in one of their movies?

matter if they can totally morph from one character to another depending on what the script calls for. What does matter is that they can perform acts that call for out-of-the-ordinary physical skill and ability without getting hurt or endangering others.

Of course, that endangering part is sometimes easier said than done. No matter how good they are at what

GO FOR IT IF. . .

You've never met a sports challenge you didn't like.

- - - - - - - - - - - - -

You don't like going down the smallest of hills on your bike.

FORGET ABOUT IT IF. . .

they do, when you are taking some of the risks stunt people typically take when filming things like high-speed chases and explosions, accidents do happen.

But accidents are less likely to occur with a stunt professional than with the average person because, for one thing, stunt people tend to be in tip-top physical condition, and they work hard to get this way. For another thing, stunt people get to be stunt people because they are awesome at what they do, whether their specialty is gymnastics, martial arts, or horseback riding. Some are so specialized that they are known for high falls, car chases, or fights. Of course, more skills mean more jobs, so experienced stunt people tend to build up a wide range of skills over time.

Go Online to Find Out More!

Find out more about how stunt people work at http://entertainment. howstuffworks.com/ stuntmen.htm.

More Scary Jobs

Some scary jobs are easy to overlook. That's because you see people do them every day. Some of these jobs seem so ordinary that you probably don't give a minute's thought to the risk these people take. Other jobs are so extraordinary that it's easy to forget that the people putting themselves in danger to do them are real people with families who care about them. So, whether the job they do seems ordinary or extraordinary, be sure to give two thumbs up for the people gutsy enough to do the kinds of work you'll read about here.

Driver

Driving a taxicab is dangerous? Yep. So is driving a truck or, for that matter, even chauffeuring a fancy limousine. So dangerous, in fact, that when you put all the jobs that involve operating moving vehicles together, they account for more than half of the fatal injuries that occur at work in the United States each year.

Of course, if you've ever ridden in a taxi during rush hour in a big city or felt the whoosh of a Mack truck zooming past your family's car on the highway, you can probably imagine that the potential for disaster is always lurking just around the corner.

So, when you start driving, take it easy when you see these professional drivers out and about. Give them a break (or brake, as the need may be). And, don't forget to buckle up!

Emergency Rescue Worker

Some poor sap lost his way in a snowstorm on the side of a remote mountain. A hiker fell and broke her leg out in the wilderness. Or, closer to home, someone falls off a ladder while painting his house and needs help now!

Lucky for them—and thanks to a variety of different types of emergency rescue workers—help is on the way. You see some of these emergency workers rushing through your neighborhood in ambulances or fire trucks with sirens blaring. Others work for the military or national park service and are standing by at a moment's notice to jump in a helicopter, a Coast Guard speed boat, or, in some cases, onto the back of a horse, to go wherever they need to go to save the day.

The job title says it all. Anytime you put the words *emergency* and *rescue* together, you know there will be enough danger nearby to keep the adrenaline pumping.

Fisherman

The world consumes more than 156 tons of seafood every year and, in case you haven't noticed, those fish don't find their way to the dinner table by someone standing on a beach calling, "Here, fishy, here." Someone has to go get them.

And that's exactly what fishermen (and women!) do. Whether it's wild salmon in Alaska, crab in Venezuela, or shrimp in China, fishermen all over the world head out to the open sea to find them. It doesn't take much imagination to figure out that anything you do on an ocean is significantly more dangerous than if you do it on dry land.

Death by drowning is the first danger that comes to mind. But, then, by it's very nature, fishing is hard, physically demanding work, so there's always a risk of getting hurt using some of the heavy equipment. And, of course, there's always Mother Nature and her fickle ways with weather to think about. You never know when a storm might come up fast.

Oceanographer

If it's not the weather, or the water, it's the sharks making work interesting and sometimes more than a little dangerous for oceanographers and other marine scientists conducting research at sea. Although much of their work is done sitting in front of a computer in a comfortable laboratory, oceanographers generally spend more time than the average person aboard ships, boats, and other sea-worthy vessels.

Depending on the nature of their work, they may even find it necessary to don scuba gear and take the plunge underwater to get up close and personal with the sea creatures they are studying. But even though these scientists sometimes find themselves a little too close for comfort to some of the ocean's more dangerous elements, they don't worry too much about sharks.

After all, the odds of getting killed by a shark are just one in 300 million.

Surgeon

They make it look so easy on TV. A sick person comes to the hospital. A doctor scrubs up, cuts the person open, fixes the problem, and presto, an hour later the patient goes home with his very relieved family, and the doctor freshens up for a hot date with the cute resident (that's a doctor in training) who assisted with the surgery.

But, think about it. You're a doctor. Very sick people come to you with life-threatening problems and trust you to fix them. The problem could be any one of a million things. Not only do you have to figure out what the problem really is, but you may also have to perform intricate surgical procedures on organs that you can only get to with a surgical knife. Every day, people trust you not to kill them when you do things that, under ordinary circumstances, would be very dangerous. It's not like you'd want just anybody poking around in your brain, would you?

Test Pilot

If the idea of hurtling through the sky at breathtaking speeds in a heavy metal tube filled with people (airline passengers) isn't scary enough for you, what about doing what a test pilot does? Test pilots get paid by the military and aerospace companies to find out all the things that could possibly go wrong with their new aircrafts.

What's so scary about that? Well, sometimes the only way to find out is to actually take off and push the aircraft to its limits. It's a task that is easier said than done when you're flying a super secret, ultra-sleek fighter jet so high and so fast that the world blurs by at 11 miles a minute.

One of the world's most famous test pilots was Chuck Yeager, a pilot who was the first person to break the sound barrier (which means he flew a plane faster than the speed at which sound travels). He did this, among many other daring aerial feats, back in 1947.

Wild Animal Trainer

Maybe you've seen them at work at a zoo or circus: those seemingly fearless people who make their way into a lion (or tiger or elephant) cage and, with a few simple commands, get them to do all kinds of incredible tricks. There they are jumping through hoops, balancing on balls, even eating right out of the trainer's hands!

Smart wild animal trainers always keep in mind that it doesn't matter how much training a wild animal gets, it is still a wild animal by nature. Just because the lion has done what the trainer has told it to do 1,000 times doesn't guarantee that it will do it 1,001 times. Just ask Roy Horn of the famous Siegfried

and Roy magician and training duo. Horn, a man with 30 years of experience working with wild cats, was badly injured during a Las Vegas performance when a seven-year-old white tiger named Montecore, whom he had trained since he was a cub, mauled him and then dragged him offstage right in front of a horrified audience. Fortunately, Roy survived and recovered.

Window Washer

What's so scary about washing windows, you ask? Well, it depends on where the windows are located. If you're washing the windows of, say, a fast food joint, no sweat. The scariest thing you are likely to encounter there is a big blob of ketchup smeared around the glass. Yikes! For a minute there you thought it was blood!

On the other hand, it's another story if the window is located on the 32nd floor of a Manhattan skyscraper and the only way to get to it is from the outside while standing on a narrow window-washing platform that's connected to motorized scaffold cables that allow it to move up and down very tall buildings. It's a good thing that the use of special harnesses, lifebelts, controls, and other safety equipment is required by strict laws designed to protect those who keep the world's highest windows sparkling clean.

It doesn't happen often but when all those back-up systems fail, most people aren't as lucky as Manhattan window washer Alcides Moreno, who fell 47 stories and lived to tell about it in 2007.

Real People, Scary Jobs

Who is it that does all these scary jobs? People. Everyday, ordinary people with families and friends, and neighbors and pets. People with the courage to go after their wildest dreams and people willing to conquer their fears. These people have discovered that when there is a job to do, the only thing to do is get to it and do it. They have decided that the challenge and importance of their work outweigh the risks they take. After all, when it comes right down to it, the only thing they have to fear is fear itself.

PEOPLE PROFILE 1: Nicholas Patrick, Astronaut

It's almost easier to describe what Mission Specialist Nicholas Patrick doesn't do than to try to describe everything he does do in his work at NASA. Patrick is a very well-educated

engineer who can pilot more than 20 types of airplanes and helicopters. He's an astronaut and an aquanaut (the underwater version of an astronaut). He's been to outer space and he serves as a voice between mission control on earth and astronauts in space (that's called a capsule communicator or cap comm in NASA lingo). Not to mention, he is helping to design *Orion*, the spacecraft of the future.

Patrick started training to be an astronaut in 1998. Like other astronauts in training, he spent a lot of time in the classroom and also in sophisticated laboratory and simulated space environments. He even spent 10 days living in an underwater habitat called Aquarius. There he got the chance to find out what it's like to live without gravity 24/7, plus he found out that, yes indeed, he could live in an isolated, confined space without freaking out. Ultimately, he passed every challenge NASA threw at him and he was selected to go to space.

Patrick's big day finally arrived on December 9, 2006. That's when he and seven fellow astronauts took off aboard Space Shuttle *Discovery* to link up with the International Space Station. Their mission involved three main tasks: deliver two tons of food, water, and equipment; swap out a shuttle astronaut for one who had already spent six months on the Space Station; and wire the space station with better electrical systems. Two weeks and 5.3 million miles later, Patrick and the team were back on earth to fearlessly tackle more NASA challenges.

To find out more about Patrick's adventures in space, go online to http://www.nasa.gov/mission_pages/shuttle/shuttlemissions/archives/sts-116.html.

PEOPLE PROFILE 2: Tamiko Bogad, Bomb Squad Technician

If it's scary to work on a bomb squad in a major city, can you imagine how scary it would be to work on one in a military war zone? First Sergeant Tamiko Bogad knows firsthand what it's like and says the thing she most feared was that she would not be able to get a bomb rendered (or defused) before someone got hurt.

As one of very few female bomb squad technicians with the U.S. Army's Explosive Ordinance Disposal (EOD) Unit, Bogad served two tours of duty in Iraq and one in Afghanistan. The situation she encountered in Afghanistan was a bomb squad technician's ultimate challenge: The Soviet Union had deserted millions of military munitions after they were defeated in an earlier war. Her unit's job was to safely destroy these weapons by blowing them up. It was like the world's biggest fireworks display! She admits that it was fun to get rid of them knowing that no one would ever be able to use them to hurt other people.

The situation in Iraq wasn't so fun. That's because terrorists use homemade bombs as their weapon of choice to wreak havoc. There were many occasions when she had to defuse bombs right on the spot. When that happened, she says it was like everything stopped and the only thing she could hear was the sound of her own breathing inside her protective suit.

Now that she's back on American soil, Bogad shares her experiences to train other bomb squad technicians, and leads a team of 177 soldiers and civilians who provide support for all of the Army's EOD units. She also continues to lead the way for more women to follow in her footsteps in a pacesetting military career.

PEOPLE PROFILE #3: Tony Hawk, Extreme Sports Pro

When he was a kid, Tony Hawk's mother called him "challenging." His teachers kindly called him "gifted." By his own admission, he was a "terrible youth."

When he was 12, thanks to a gift from his brother, Hawk found a place to channel all his energy and competitiveness in skateboarding. By 14 he was a professional skateboarder, and by 16 he was considered the best skateboarder in the world. Hawk is credited with the invention of more than 80 impressive aerial skateboard tricks including the Stalefish, Madonna, and McHawk. But his biggest claim to fame was being the first skateboarder in history to land the 900 (making two and a half rotations in the air before landing back on the ground), which he did on national TV during the 1999 X Games.

Even so, no one can say that the world famous Hawk was an overnight success. He's seen more than his share of ups and downs, and setbacks and injuries. But, these days, after years of competition and keeping with it, Hawk is head of an enormous extreme sports empire. In addition to lots of product endorsements and public appearances, Hawk is associated with a whole line of DVDs and electronic games, books, clothes, and, of course, skateboards. He also runs the Tony Hawk Foundation, which, among other things, gives away money to create public skateboard parks in low-income neighborhoods.

No one is more surprised than Hawk himself that he's been able to make a living from skateboarding. You can find out more about Hawk's amazing accomplishments at http://www.tonyhawk.com.

PEOPLE PROFILE #4: Debi Radisch, Forensic Pathologist

Even though her official title is associate chief medical examiner for the state of North Carolina, Dr. Debi Radisch likes to think of herself as a problem-solver. She sees each of the 250 or so cases she works on each year as a chance to solve a mystery or figure out a puzzle.

All of the cases Dr. Radisch works on have one thing in common: a dead body. Her job is to figure out how each person died. Sometimes the clues make things pretty obvious: They were in a fatal car accident or were murdered. But she still has to figure out the exact nature of the injuries and fill out lots of official reports.

Other times, the cause of death isn't so clear. For instance, one time police found the body of a young man lying in a creek underneath a highway and didn't know how he got there. The plot thickened when police found his car parked on the side of the highway above the creek. Things got even more interesting when they learned that the dead man was training to become a police officer. Had he been the victim of a crime?

Putting all the pieces together, Dr. Radisch suggested that he might have stopped to help someone on the other side of the highway. Since it was late at night, he might not have seen a gap in the road between the median on his side of the road and the one where the stranded person's car was parked. Based on all these clues and the types of his injuries, Dr. Radisch concluded that he simply fell to his death on his way to perform a good deed. The police agreed. Case closed. And the man's loved ones were able to find comfort knowing that he had died as a hero.

Scary Job Playground

You've read about scary jobs that other people do. Here's your chance to play around with the idea of having a scary job yourself someday. So, what do you think? Is there a scary job in your future? (Oh, and by the way, if this book doesn't belong to you, please use a separate sheet of paper to record your answers.)

⭐ Watch Out, Scary Job, Here I Come

Imagine that you're all grown up, and ready to tackle an awesome career...

Would You Do It?	Can't Wait to Try It Someday!	Maybe—If I Ever Get The Nerve!	Not A Chance!
Astronaut			
Bomb Squad Technician			
Disease Detective			
Extreme Sports Pro			
Forensic Pathologist			
Smokejumper			
Skywalker			
Spy			
Stormchaser			
Stunt Person			

✪ Mirror, Mirror on the Wall…

Which of these jobs is scariest of all?

- ◎ Driver
- ◎ Emergency Rescue Worker
- ◎ Fisherman
- ◎ Oceanographer
- ◎ Surgeon
- ◎ Test Pilot
- ◎ Wild Animal Trainer
- ◎ Window Washer

✪ Help Wanted: Brave Person for Scary Job

Pick the scariest job you can think of from these lists or from your own wild imagination. Make sure it's so scary you'd never dream of doing it yourself. But, hey, someone's got to do it. So write a "help wanted" ad trying to convince someone else to do it. Try to emphasize the positive aspects of the job without scaring them off!

✪ Hot Off the Press!

What's your idea of a perfectly scary job? Can you invent one so scary that people will want to know all about it? Now imagine yourself doing it.

Pretend that a celebrity magazine thinks your job is so cool that they want to feature you on the front cover. They asked you to write a short story about what you do. Include lots of hair-raising details and be sure to throw in a few tips on how you manage to do it without scaring yourself half to death.

✪ One More Thing…

Make a list of any good books or interesting Web sites you find to further explore scary job ideas. You can use a search engine like http://kids.yahoo.com to search for information by typing in the name of a career you'd like to know more about. Or ask your school media specialist or librarian for help finding some books.

Index

Page numbers in **bold** indicate photographs.